To Barbara

Very happy 90th!

Best wishes

Adrian + Irene

SPOILS

SPOILS

∾

JAMES BROOKES

First published in 2018
by Offord Road Books
@OffordRoadBooks

Typeset by Martha Sprackland
Printed in the UK by TJ International

ISBN 978–1–999–93040–0

1 3 5 7 9 10 8 6 4 2

for Charlotte

Contents

SPOILS

Things have the defects of their qualities

A. L. Rowse, *The English Past*

*I just don't see how a world that makes
such wonderful things could be bad*

Ariel, *The Little Mermaid*

Eschatology, Piscatology

The halotolerant crocodile
idles in brackish water like a tow truck.
Salt-glands meter in its diapsid skull;
smug fucker that the epochs couldn't kill.

How easy 'kill' then closes onto 'smile',
the lockjaw of a life that rides its luck,
knowing from hindmost teeth to jackknifed tail
Leviathan is neither fish nor mammal.

Tenulla

Summer forms its *oklad*, its dense *riza*
over (now iconic) Riva del Garda.

Driftwood fascines hold and hem the waters
which hardly lap against their bronze revetments.

Of course, we can't afford to honeymoon there
but paradise is anywhere you swim.

Water girl, so blithe against the cold
you swim until the blue tinge of your skin

shames the water; then out of water, nothing
will cheer you up, will stop you wandering.

How helpless and how fascinated I
watch you shiver, half nude, humourless,

your arms closed round your bundled legs for warmth,
fencing yourself with bundles and bundles of thoughts:

fasciculus, funiculus, your mind's
little bunch of twigs, its fragile ladder;

my silly soul still mounting up and up
and up and up and up *funiculì funiculà*.

Δευκᾰλιων

Wednesday we drank to ourselves, as is our wont:
finished the Grand Cru, vinegar, grape must,
and floated on, decanters dry as dust,
to the Propontic and the Hellespont.

Tonight looks like more rain. There is no berth
that's worth the myth with which we'll be regaled.
We thought we might repopulate the earth;
wiser counsel thankfully prevailed.

After Paul Nash's *Totes Meer*

At Passchendaele, at Dymchurch, Romney Marsh;
Dymchurch especially: chapels of mischance.
The arch sea fretting over fixed defences;
deep groynes the legions sank beneath redoubts,
sank dead march deep in reinforced concrete,
stacking absolute upon absolute
by ranks. *Serve God*
            But First Maintain the Wall.
Under the cliff, skeletal cockpit scaffold
and shark-fin empennage of a downed Heinkel,
sickly, hyperreal . . . forms with their black magenta
and orange colourings. The ancient Marsh Churches
now empty as Cain's howls brought easterly
inland to the Weald, to Iden, named
for him who once trapped Jack Cade in a garden,
desperation draining like a tide surge.

The Bronze

It came upon us like a figurehead
displacing mist. It took a fisheye lens
just to table it. Birds of every clade
had shat upon it; made a nidifice
within the hollow of its diadem.
It wore its ruin like a pinafore.
What it was meant to be, why, what amount
of toil had brought there, was beyond us.
We tried, with skill and not-a-little care,
to translate its *tabula ansata*.
But we gave up. At least we left it clean.
It had a smile. Perhaps because it meant
GOD DAMN YOU ALL TO HELL. And it was glad
that it had come. That it had come to this.

Street Party, Día de Muertos 1998

Boomtown. Later decadence. Our *danse*
macabre is still the Macarena.
Cacao Noir. Aztec Deco. New World Baroque.
The suits polygonic and sharp as any script.
Bonemeal feeds the flowers. There is no object
without a witty use we might put it to.

Sell it to me: an infinite way to chainsmoke;
cracking our knuckles to the open mic;
swigging Goldschläger in the airport lobby;
the cackle of perpetual roulette.
In this world so alive with *momento mori*
no one hears threnody. No one sees 'end of an era'.

I'm shipping out in the morning.
Crack a jeroboam over my forehead.
Frieze my puzzled look. Clad my expression in chrome.
I want to pull this moment from my coat
for anyone at any given moment.
Don't tell me *I don't really want to do that.*

Play it once, for old times' sake. Querida,
love is for the living. Let me have this dance.

Party at which Paul Dirac Doesn't Dance

for Tom Boardman

For the self that watches Werner Heisenburg dance
For the self-confessed pleasure of dancing with nice girls

For the self as void, your plus one pie-eyed on e
For the self as an identity, that might be Euler's

For the self as the set of all self-conscious selves
For the self as a word unsaid, a meal choked down

For the self of G. H. Hardy's *A Mathematician's Apology*
For the self of the 'Don Bradman as poet' analogy

For the self as the self-willed absence of Perelman
For the self as the prolific & the profligate Feynman

For the self as prime pseud, as cliché, as cargo cult
For the self as something the mind can't do without

For the self that has fully fuck-àll to do with Fermat
For the self writ too large in its own marginalia

For the self as Dirac δ function upon which
the self and its angels and axioms can dance

Birthday Party, East Cicero 1926

The gun in 'Fats' Waller's back was flat and sharp
as the brims of the hats of the four hoodlums in suits
who forced him into the car, which was also black
like the suits and the hats and the gun and the flats and sharps
on the shoddy upright at which he found himself sat
at the Hawthorne Inn and of course the house was packed
and he's surprise guest and the birthday boy's face had a scar,
the champagne bar was open and yes, sir, he can play requests.

Rue d'Odessa

for Д. X.

Imagine us run to ground in Brno, Dubrovnik,
cough-mixture-drunk, Official Secrets like teeth
loose in our gums. Imagine us two shots apiece.
I drank for us in Paris – *vodka aux épices* –
the only time that I've known you to miss a trick.
With half a brain and 3/5ths of a plan,
the Commonwealth of the UK & the Ukraine,
we promised ourselves some weekday EU panic

but Paris frankly sucks without you, Danik.
Danik, I know you're smoking Exile's Choice
in school. I know. The school's a damn U-Bähn.
We're too damn smart to stay here. Where to run?
The Café Magyar Carta? L'Hôtel Trianon?
You'll try your luck embezzling *pizdetz* goys:
He paid his Jews! Ya geddit? Paid. His. Jews.
I'll trade my Exit Visa; forge my shoes.

Love Song for an Épéeiste

Between my first thought, *gracile*, and my second,
antimasque, you have already entered

deft beneath the offered-up engagement.

To be struck thus on the fingertip, the toe,
is fatal.

There is no distinction
                              of strategy and tactics
which is all body,

my pupil follows your point like a dilettante,
the argument of a master.

How your arm retakes its own tensile strength
                                              escrimeuse,
is a pure romance. Your *prise-de-fer en seconde*

the rasping noise of your *glizade* as it lingers
in the post-bout shower; distal taper of your calf

as you appel and lunge,
each pore and each sebaceous gland your second.

Heart, too-well-guarded target, forgive my dull fingers,
the wholehearted *flèche* of my tongue tripping over itself.

Ironwork

for Fiona Brookes, chained to the gate of Buckingham Palace

The world cannot be otherwise
           than as it is; nor can it be
made otherwise by force of wish,
           or deed, or inactivity:
it draws these cooling certainties
           from each of us. Magnetic north
allows the compass. Rules are rules;
           there's nothing else to rail against.
Remanded into such a state
           we put trust in the tensile strength
that policy has coalesced
           in something human, something made
to be impassive, maybe just.
           The measured world meanwhile is full
of everything that we allow,
           of law and bylaw, bar and gate.
Between the upright parallels,
           it may be that you see a face
working its way from rage to hope,
           a world that is not finished yet
of rightful silence, of held breath.
           The blush that's iron in the flesh
troops its colour. With no release,
           from core out to capillary,
each cell has pled its own small case,
           the iron rising unappeased,
defendant of an inward grace,
           restrained, impossible to police.

After Christopher Nevinson's *Any Wintry Afternoon in England*

How it's always overcast in paradise.
Or in *A Flooded Trench on the Yser, 1916*

the sky's entrenched, the trench an inverse lightning
laid flat between two continents of ice.

Here it is as lightning, as a man
kicking a football. The ball is now a shellburst

of sun void at eclipse. The man's black boot,
howitzer freeze-framed; legs searchlit elevations,

snapshot in front of smokestack, steam train, slope roofs
rain-scored like fresh scratches on dull metal.

How it's the same old heavy weather still,
autrefois, among the nerves of the world,

all angels vortices of the same stripe
playing out the derby above Eden.

On a Visit to a Frontline Service

The squaddie with the pince-nez bruise
that blackens both his eyes

gives one great sympathetic grin
to humour, to despise.

His jawline's lantern razor-rash,
his flash of downlit chin,

his complete and bloody cheek is
still 1945:

posterboy of swept fag ash
and cheery hardluck charm

whose Brodie tin hat grinned the same,
bold faced, 'LABOUR FOR HIM'.

That ringfenced smile for when he jokes
the meaning of defeat is

rolling a Help for Heroes sock
over a prosthesis.

Lines, waiting in the car park while she gets her prescription filled

A sycamore raises keloid scars in tarmac,
a root system that may not be overridden.
This universe: god–heat–sink, info–midden,
how its Riemannian manifolds flex, not crack
with the weight and the levity of every 'if'
as though some motive force beneath it all
is forcing out the answer *life! life! life!*
from stars sending their everything to **/dev/null**

Charges from the Douce Apocalypse

Passim, the fork-tailed
freehousing red lion
of de Montfort, its coat
now turned inside out
in a towering whitewash.

Lance-jack stripes, de Clare
spilt claret chevrons
armed and blazoned
like the very devil:
between three frogs proper
on a field of gore,
a dry river of gold.

Summer's an obligate season;
think fluke, think tick, think cuckoo,
think broods of mosquito
-vectored plasmodium.

Come, five-hearted
houseguest, earthworm,
come, aorist,
that my flat pulse
enrich your each
aortic arch.

Tissue Section, Frontal Lobe
(Dementia)

The body's notes towards Chaos Theory:
hindwings of a Queen of Spain fritillary,
ventral side up; unfinished tracery
of chancel window; blind spot gallery;
clean bite mark of a strange maxillary
dentition. Crown of a family tree.

After Graham Sutherland's *Thorn Head*

Spur rowels, caltrops, claw-set within a sickle, a gimbal, a beak.
As always: arms race. Crescent and cruciform tropes
so at each others' throats that no one might tell
where the bights of their knot become integral,
where their working end is found.
                                        Black Redstarts
holiday here nonetheless, are almost exclusive
to urban wasteland and to brownfield sites:
season ticket holders, they sing the hook
that'll catch in your head all summer; travelling fans
of London since before Woolwich Arsenal
rehomed from Highbury to the Emirates
hard by the lanthorn-head of Finsbury Park Mosque.

Christmas Party with Admiral Nelson
at Fonthill Abbey

You will now think it an odd coincidence:
amidst the huzzahing multitude
a person who had attended him
at the time he had lost an arm
and had assisted with the amputation.
The noble Admiral beckoned him upstairs,
took him by the hand with a present in his own;
as the man withdrew, he took from his bosom
a piece of lace
which he had torn from the sleeve of the amputated arm
declaring he would preserve it till his last breath.

An Instance of Privilege

These fingers, the archaeologists of a goose,
at Christmas ravish the carcass for choicest parts
– *spolia opima* – liver, spleen, neck, pluck;
each toroid corpuscle, each erythrocyte
valued. Retract the digits, captive bolts,
from the cavity; divide the giblets,
prime the gas hob to receive the goose lights,
put tongue to copper palate. So the cook
shall cherish and itemise and do no harm.
It seems the flesh neither abets nor halts.

Sylvia Pankhurst in
Addis Ababa

Beyond the unfenced
garden of the grace
and favour residence
the slums and the palace
almost make sense
of every choice
painting the days dense
with eucalyptus
and the work never finished.

Augustus Egg Buys
The Death of Chatterton

The delicacy of his breeches,
the crotch, centrefold
in seamless lavender
above the bedsheet's rough stitches
(though everyone knows
what arsenic does to the bowels).

This kid is a goldmine.
Patently endowed
with the good sense
of his gunsmith forebears,
Augustus reckons
the reproduction rights will be worth a fortune.

Smugglerius

Here is the resurrected criminal's
exquisite corpse as human apogee,
in their second body, this clean copy
modelled in the pose of the Dying Gaul.

Muscular écorché, without the pain
in skinfuls that this dressing-up undid:
not blood delineating those faint veins
but sugarsoap and Jeyes Fluid.

Flet victus, said wise Livy, *victor interriit*:
the conquered weeps, the conqueror's undone.
The barbarous exists to be made polite,
the individual made to redeem the culture.

Christabel Pankhurst
in Santa Monica

Bereft of good fights,
one only defeats
death; dying upright
in one's chosen seat.

Song

in memoriam Peter Reading

Why are you waiting for death's slow ministration?
A curule chair seats —— —— the sarcoma;
—— —— perjures himself for the premiership.
Why are you waiting for death's slow ministration?

Party at Nero's with Britannicus

Immodest, feckless and effete,
the epicure can still defeat
the stoic. He may have to cheat.

We drank from murrhine cups so rare
we couldn't even be sure where
our host had sourced them: Derbyshire

Blue John, or maybe amethyst;
their colour the crushed varicose
of a chokehold or a love-bite bruise.

Amethyst will protect the lush
from leglessness when on the lash
the way permanganate of potash

is supposed to purify water.
That's how the poisoner Locusta
works around a hired wine-taster:

her waiter pours the water, while we wait,
shifting from buttock to buttock in our seats,
to drink the same wine, some thinned down, some neat.

Fetter Lane Sword

I like to leave my fingerprints on gold
    and print my brief reflection in the world
        more real. The dirt beneath the fingernail
        of silver and lead sulphide niello.

        Here, sense and apprehension are enrolled:
        gilt garniture and brokenbladed sword
of nearby truth and justice (not to scale).
Blindfold, baroque; what else could we afford?

Battersea Shield

Crêpe-paper thin and therefore votive – hence
its spoiled form in the river's secret ballot.
Riveted beneath its low relief,
its chambers fixed with cloisonné enamel
cracked–upholstery–leather–red; expense
to turn the eye and beggar the belief

and stand upright on palanquins and pallets
such consequence as none of you can trammel.
So please you, think: what offered no defence
in life survives the microbe and the maggot.
Those wishes that have yet to come to grief
invite you to your own irrelevance.

To a Semiconductor

Charge-carrier of quantum magic,
electron-sieving crystal lattice

whose pristine epitaxial growth
when handled by a nitrile glove

is mirror-perfect. Gallium
arsenide in doped silicon

etched anisotropically,
you are my kind of poetry:

a demiurge's legerdemain,
resistance lost, conductance gained,

giving our spoil of earth's abstruse
flickerings of such brief impulse

diffusion – we could call it scope;
complexity in place of hope.

Éminence Grise

Thin like brook-water
    — Pound, 'Yeux Glauques'

I liked the portrait:
light foot but heavyset;
those cheeks; eyelids
stye-blemished, thick
membranes of brocade velvet;
how tired, splendid
the embouchure, quick
the flash of teeth, *ad
unguem*. I mean, imagine
living like that?
Nothing to gainsay,
no one to outwit . . .

Cadaver Synod

On the banks of the Tiber Pope Formosus,
fresh from his tribunal, performs posthumous
miracles. You too could be gameshow famous!

Satan upon his throne of realgar,
in his cupped palm a globus cruciger
of Unicum, anticipates the year

when syphilis resists all penicillin
and sees us first retreat to Salvarsan
then pills of white mercury cut with laudanum.

But try not to worry. If you worry, just
think of the future's warehouse, full of promise.
Yes, there's a *chance* that, like Emperor Galerius,

you'll succumb to septic shock from Fournier's
gangrene (don't Google that!). Still, your cadaver
could be exquisite. You are very clever:

across your windscreen's blank Cartesian plane
the streetlights plot regression toward mean.
Your world may be grotesque but not obscene.

Afterparty with Bruce Chatwin
in Dahomey

Wake up in a country that no longer exists,
effervescent as a banker's draft,
immune to counterfeit as a cowrie shell.
Sweat in reams of *appliqué* cloth,

acacia in the ditches of the forts.
Horreur du domicile. Home is a fetish,
requested, required; a poor phylactery,
a passport no longer worth its watermark.

Adela Pankhurst
in Wahroonga

Left, right, left, right:
what else can one do

when life militates
against one so,

the soup bowls fill
with cigarette ash,

and it's only fools
and saints that ask

not to be right,
not to be left?

Final Memo from the Ministry

Tinted soda-lime, the windows' noticeboard
shows many states of occupied withdrawal:
the forest vaults reconstituted from Hansard,
the muffled squares, the suffragan cathedrals

shady beneath the branches of Bastard Service.
Half the staff already gone –
why? We were busy, busy in every office:
Sidney Street, Runnymede, Tyburn . . .

But we have officially outlasted our purpose.
And where we are to go, no one supposes.
Variegations of mosaic virus
have ruined our imported Paestum roses.

After Glynn Williams' *The Flowering of the English Baroque*

Silliness shall conspire to break our hearts
like something in Purcell; his puckish last work:
the weird, imperial tomfoolery
of 'Bonduca'.   Festooned putto faces
of jolly Jack o'th'Green druids
remixed with hornpipes and contrapuntal folk.
May Day nonsense, may it happen again,
every season's moment to blow your mind:
mine was Jeff Buckley covering Dido's Lament
(Meltdown Festival, 1995)
ragged, impossible, off the top of his head.

Song for a Dark Queen

i.m. Rosemary Sutcliff 1920-1992

in all that red havoc, I had my harp again
as wonderful as the sudden starry opening of a flower
among the stink and filth of a knacker's yard.
I would have given my own gift of song to have my hands round
the throat of the man who had driven hers away. And I snapped the
   twisted
horsehair under my fingers, cutting my hand so that the red
sprang out in a thin line.
Blood spurted out over her hand. She looked at her hand and smiled;
the first time that I had seen her smile in many moons;
she who gives all in life and takes all things back in death.
She is the love of a man and a woman and the child born from it;
she is in the corn that ripens to harvest, and in the seed corn
that demands blood shed into the furrows before it quickens;
she is in the stoop of a falcon on a leveret cowering in the long grass;
she is in battle and the deaths of men.
'I will make you your song of a Queen's Victories', I said.
Have we not learned to wait, we whose life is the corn and the herds?
Who can hurry the growth of the seed-corn in the ground
or the young in the belly of its dam?
Hush, my harp, for the time is not yet, for singing;
and bright dark and terrible the song will be.

'Part of Your World'

The more people who want to sing the song, the better it is for all of us
— Jodi Benson

When the simple joy of an object transforms my body
from its own wondrous cavernousness to one that echoes
  with others
that might just be my subject – only
I wonder if that was what Howard Ashman was thinking.
Was he even there in his body when he heard Jodi
working out her way between singing and speaking?
The virus killing him even then, but who cares,
Jodi's Ariel and there's no more need for such things,
the mind, the body, the world already there
in that gesture I learnt as a child from her avatar
of longing who became my focus of longing –
I still close my fingers plaintively on the air
that might as well be water or song – it's who I am singing.
I too want to be where the people are.

Stag Party at Blo' Norton

This weekend smells of sandalwood
    and bacon grease.
The sun cannot contain its own content:
    a ball of orpiment
added to molten cannonballing lead
    droplets freefalling down a Shot
Tower's oesophagus
    to make more perfect spheres.
Trapshooting, we have filled the morning
    with buckshot
and splintered clay. Pull and release.

Last night we plucked the gravel from my thigh
    and scotched
the wound with ethanol. Let
    this scar not fade,
however much it soothes under the hot
    shower's open torment,
falling once more with the sun, outside
    to occident
with round-headed rampion, calqued
    forget-me-not
here with me and here with me too, heartsease
    called love-in-idleness,
or, in Sussex, 'kiss me'.

ANTIGEORGICS

'six of the worst miles in England, which miles terminate but a few hundred yards before you enter Horsham . . . in short, it is a most villainous tract. After quitting it, you enter a forest; but a most miserable one; and this is followed by a large common, now enclosed, cut up, disfigured, spoiled, and the labourers all driven from its skirts.'

— William Cobbett, *Rural Rides*

De Excidio et Conquestu Britanniae

I see the goddess Sussex as my wife
at Peacehaven, where the Prime Meridian
pits time against itself. In her left fist
she holds a cache of scalene arrowheads,
the Horsham points, those hollow pygmy flints
the first things made on this three-cornered rock.
Her right hand sprouts a billhook's murderous curve,
a pruning hook repurposed as a polearm,
its ferrule like a tentspike in the lumbar
of ruined earth, and there beneath her feet
she has shredded the Rescript of Honorius
who told her she must look to her own defence,
DEA INDOMITA   DEA HASTATRIX
spearlady like the wildcat in the furze,
queen of the grey-green eye as though she fixed
to cleave the yoke of brutishness,
our simple-minded people of forms.
Her hair arterial spray against a coast
alien as any glimpsed by Pytheas
where the Arun and the Adur soak
the forest of Anderida,
strombolo lignite scabs the beach,
disposed contaminated sharps
in heathgrass, matgrass, hairgrass, sedge,
the choked apothecariat
of ruined green, brown and milkglass
bottles stamped NOT TO BE TAKEN
not woad but vitrum, Caesar's word,
high watermark and bleeding edge,
an offer of spoils, an apocalypse.
Hers is a country I might believe and die in.

Tapsel Gate, Jevington

Pivot the year;   the cold revolving door
half-sticking in the frost. The weather lifts
over the South Downs, bearing as before
its poison pen love letters, stalker's gifts,
and moves inland to numb the limbs of Horsham.
Sussex never rowed its own coracle;
it might have once careered an essedum.
No henge at equinox its oracle,
just grand and petulant intransigence.
Patriotism? No. I don't lack the lingo –
no matter what I might offer in my defence
these jangled syllables stay the chains of jingo –
but can I say aloud that my sort spoiled the world
without that sly inflection of self-pity
I cannot shift for money or for love?
The Sussex motto is *we wunt be druv*.

Covert Pastoral

The Death's-head Hawkmoth, *Acherontia atropos*
screaming like a Stuka, like a loomworks:
buried alive in smoked hive's propolis.
From Parry's Jerusalem to Holst's Thaxted,

from croft to terrace, from distaff to suffrage,
from Sussex bucolic to Sussex democratic,
bugonia's not exactly a bygone era.
Poets keep fucking writing about bees.

Bog Asphodel

Sun-up, first Sunday after Candlemas. I took the corpse road
through first frost, vision prickled with lens flare as though I'd taken
a blow to the head or been dead drunk and only just come to.
I couldn't pick out the orange flowers of *Narthecium*
ossifragum, that'll brittle the bones of the yearling lambs,
the Lancashire asphodel, that which ought not to do down here.
I well know the flare of a corpse candle to be no such thing,
a barn owl's bioluminescent wingtip, its barrel roll
over the hollow of an elm crippled by honey fungus
smearing my path with the enzyme 'luciferase'.
To Warnham's living lychgate, then, its arch of thickening yew
like the new year: not death but a vital and lustrous darkness.
On the way back, a hare shone in the narthex of its form.

Greensand Ridge

Green, the high watermark on the cell wall
in debtors' gaol; a sickly lichen pall
of green, arsenical; a Paris Green.
Some things persist. Some things do not come clean

with Fuller's earth. Assoil us, then, spoilsport
Earth, underwriter, lender of last resort,
give us your green back, sordid antidote,
dark liquidity, promissory note.

Bloomery

When Pastor Levett, vicar and rector at Buxted,
cast the first British field piece and became
gunstonemaker-in-chief to the king's majesty
he was fired by Cranmer for breach of canon law –
then reinstated out of expediency.
This was more tradition than innovation:

soft southerners in the beginning made any old iron
as far west in the Weald as Broadfield, Crawley.
When Caesar came, the locals fashioned hobnails
for jackboots up and down arterial Stane Street;
they stamped the tiles for *Classis Britannica*.
The rose of Sussex was the bloomer,

its orange flower that yellows at a breath
from hand-, then pedal-bellows, then the mills
seeding the county with names of industry –
Furnace Pond, Slag Meadow, Culver Wood –
and though the coke-fuelled Midlands killed that life
(*ultima ratio regum* follows the money)

the forests of the Weald would still be culled
to meet our flourishing need. A mill may last,
at best, perhaps two hundred working years,
so by the time Blake pens Jerusalem
the view from Felpham is green and pleasant land;
the garden to invite trespassing souls.

Agrimony

A volatile oil and a bitter principle,
a salve to fresh cuts; 'musket-shot-water'
or *eau d'arquebusade*, if you prefer;
from the cocklebur, sticklewort, or church steeple.

Drayton's herb, by the all-heal hereafter spelt
a Sussex panacea, a dyslexic's nightmare,
possibly 'alimony' or 'angry money', if you prefer.
Apotropaic, like almost everything else.

Mayday

Devil's-bit scabious and lady's bedstraw:
the downland dressed up like its Emperor.
Each spear of the host of grass wears a maypole's splendour.

The Battle of Lewes. Richard, Earl of Cornwall,
self-styled 'King of the Romans and Always August'
cowers on the meal floor of a windmill
and looks out on the sweep of de Montfort's banners:

he saisede the mulne for a castel,
with hare sharpe swerdes he grounde the stel—
he wende that the sailes were mangonel.

A prayer has caught his lips like the faintest breeze
and the wheels within turn, slow, on the last of his hope.
The body is chaff and God into it breathes
the air's inconstancy, the swallow's plea for wings.
He grasps for any weapon that might come to hand.

'I see men as trees suffering'

Under Christ's Hospital sycamores
Macnutt, deviser of Ximenean rules,
taught the root and branch to young Keith Douglas:
'acer' for sharp, 'acies' for battle line.

Sussex was there, neither one thing nor the other,
the sergeant's singular encomium
to Capt. Douglas: 'I like you sir,
you're shit or bust'. I would that we all were.

Black Narcissus

Tight shot and vista of Himalayan Sussex,
by which of course I mean mad, bad Kathleen Byron –
her fever-pale cheeks, lust-bleached eyes, red-rimmed eyelids,
unholy touch of rouge, fresh wound of lipstick –
and Lower Beeding's invasion of rhododendrons
punishing Powell & Pressburger's Technicolor palette.

Not subtle, but subtlety's not what I'm looking for here –
just the cigarette-burn cuemarks on the fire hazard
of film base guncotton; nitrocellulose washed with camphor
and flecked like a photo-negative of ancient stars.
Beneath the crude white austerity of her nun's habit
the controlled detonation of English rose Deborah Kerr's hair.

Barn Conversion

July and the two bindweeds are in blossom.
The haymaking is over now but not long.
Sussex expressing its kenotic ethic,
its boughs spare, just roughed with lichen.

The long lanes to Whitings Farm; Hopkin's Emmaus
half-derelict; rather a fool's paradise.
'Seductive country, that Sussex', Walter Pater called it.
Platter-shaped stars, jotted with light and shadow.

Loosestrife

Squills and jonquils fucking with the golf course,
a provincial sinkhole; uniquely clipped siliquae
seeded through the fairway. I could cavil and quillet
all day, but there's loosestrife to be had
in the flesh–damp beneath the razorwire fence.
A name is no harmless thing; a name is an arms race.

but I misread 'procurator' for 'provocateur'
so what hope do I have among spadix, corymb, catkin,
an inflorescence ranged against a skyline
both of which bear unchecked proliferations?
Where is the stolen birdie of the ninth?
Who had the eagle of Calleva clip-winged and buried?

Bellis perennis

Boundless, inimical as a glacier's head,
push on, Sussex. Keep pushing that envelope,
past the last outpost, past Queen Elizabeth Land,
past help and past caring, Alexandria Eschate,

Ultima Thule. Past farthest, past uttermost.
Nuclear winter may yet become your keynote
speech. Cryogenics may yet work. Donate
any perishable organs; the rest is death's escheat.

Wild Garlic

Not ransoms but 'ramsons' – the pungent alliums
not unlike chives; good news for your court bouillon
but bad news for your courtship. Here they thrive:
bocage country. Capability wilderness.
Rubblework, breastwork, bulwark, counterscarp country.
Hack country. Slash and burn subsistence country.
Chevauchée, dynastic squabble country.
Weed-cramped, pre-ravelin country. Quarterstaff country.
Brawn and bowstave-thewed country.
Myelin-sheathed, fibre optic broadband country.
Metastasised country. Coeval woodcraft and warcraft.

Fail-deadly

A riven tree stump, its growth rings slick with rain:
the guilloche patterns cut by a rose-engine lathe
and bound in translucent enamel like Fabergé's eggs.

In temples and fanes like this, in sapwood, in heartwood,
the deathwatch beetle hides its recusancy,
its precious doomsday devices.

The hairs on its legs and back look fire-gilded,
an amalgam of gold and volatised mercury
adhering to each tiny filament.

Its ticking is not like a watch but syncopated;
the misfiring of that two-stroke jalopy moped
Giles scudded across the fields, Warnham to Slinfold

with me, riding pillion deadweight on the mudguard
clenched and crooked-of-limb, sincerely at prayer,
my heartbeat an echo of tell-tale vacancy

that brings to mind the deathwatch beetle's news:
the consecrated host is in its pyx;
the outboard motor idles on the Styx.

Antigeorgic

Sussex in excelsis,
　　　in midwinter blazon:
deciduous bronze;
　　　patinated evergreen;
fire-grimed iron;
　　　colostrum-hued Horsham stone.
The newborn soils muslin
　　　with rich meconium,
dark as wrapped silage
　　　but almost without perfume.
The roundheaded rampion
　　　biding beneath loam.
Rejoice then, my martlet,
　　　your county calls you home.
Rejoice then, my county,
　　　your failure calls you home.

After Robin Fleming's
Britain After Rome

Spelt and flax and pretty little pests
surviving in the fields. Still many years
before the old accoutrements of power
(shields with polychrome bosses, filigree
horses the colour of swans, marten pelt coats,
the highly restrictive social practices,
organised warfare, the patronage of bars,
great men having slaves and personal poets)
at last begin to build a usable past
out of the Bronze Age barrows of Slonk Hill:
the ring-ditches-turned-to-rubbish-tips backfilled,
surrounded with a squared circle enclosure,
congeries of duty-burdened rustics
kowtowing again to new men-on-the-make
skilled at appropriating other people's
dead for their own theatrical backdrop,
horizons closed with blankets of dark earth.

High Weald

As in a weapon, drum fed, or high yield.
Like dried nelumbo seedpods rattling
whack-a-mole ogive warheads,
or fat grubs in their silos of propolis,

each one a chambered round, a bracelet charm
in the many-windowed gibbet of Montfaucon,
and Sussex is at my back, brandishing the welkin:
outgunned, archaic, obsolete, suddenly winning.

Come Round at Last

on the birth of Emily Rose Sawala

I went first to my histories and found
you entirely without precedent there,
more gorgeous than Bronzino's manticore
and sure enough a somewhat loftier strain
among the grotesque taxons. Little one,
eclogue of strange nucleotides, you're here –
that lovely catlick of gold is only hair
high on your fontanelles, not halo, not mane.
But still, could you mollify my lionlimbs
with your vivid joy, and be the vivid joy,
set goodness within the orb of your wide eye
and by your especial grace and mere motion
untrouble the world entire with a yawn
to all and singular whom these presents shall come?

Acknowledgements

Thanks are due to the editors of the following journals and publications in which some versions of these poems have previously appeared: *Ambit, Eborakon, Litmus, The Next Review, Oxford Poetry, POETRY* (Chicago), *Map: Poems after William Smith's Geological Map of 1815* (Worple Press, 2015), *The Tree Line* (Worple Press, 2017).

I am grateful to Peter Carpenter, John Clegg, David Harsent, Emily Hasler, Sarah Howe, Chris Larkin, Chris Miller, Roddy Lumsden, Toby Martinez de las Rivas, Ruth Padel, Declan Ryan and Robert Selby for advice and encouragement.

Special thanks as ever to Peter Longshaw and to Tom Boardman, to my family and to Charlotte Newman.